LIGHTNING
BOLT
BOOKS™

Can You Tell a Giganotosaurus from a Spinosaurus?

Buffy Silverman

Lerner Publications Company
Minneapolis

Lerner Publications Company
A division of Lerner Publishing Group, Inc.
241 First Avenue North
Minneapolis, MN 55401 U.S.A.

Website address: www.lernerbooks.com

Library of Congress Cataloging-in-Publication Data

Silverman, Buffy.
    Can you tell a giganotosaurus from a spinosaurus? / by Buffy Silverman.
        pages   cm. — (Lightning Bolt Books™—Dinosaur Look-Alikes)
    Includes index.
    ISBN 978-1-4677-1358-0 (library binding : alkaline paper)
    ISBN 978-1-4677-1756-4 (eBook)
    1. Giganotosaurus—Juvenile literature. 2. Spinosaurus—Juvenile literature. 3. Dinosaurs—
Juvenile literature. I. Title.
    QE862.S3S4834 2014
    567.912—dc23   2012047849

Manufactured in the United States of America
1 — BP — 7/15/13

Table of Contents

Giant Hunters

Dinosaurs roamed Earth millions of years ago. Most dinosaurs ate plants. Others hunted animals.

The largest hunting dinosaurs belonged to a group called theropods. Theropods walked on two legs.

Their sharp claws helped them grab other creatures. Their sharp teeth tore up food.

Giganotosaurus and Spinosaurus were two of the largest theropods. They both had tiny arms and big bodies. But you can tell these dinosaurs apart.

Which theropod is a Giganotosaurus? Which is a Spinosaurus?

Spinosaurus was named for the tall spines on its back. Skin probably covered these spines. The spines formed a hump called a sail.

Spinosaurus means "spiny lizard."

Scientists are not sure why Spinosaurus had a sail. But they have a few ideas. Spinosaurus spread its sail like a giant fan. Its sail made the dinosaur look even bigger. So maybe the sail kept enemies away.

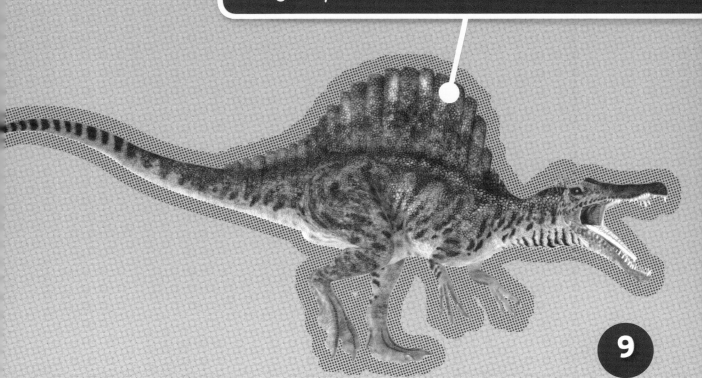

Spinosaurus's sail might have been brightly colored to attract a mate.

Spinosaurus's sail might have soaked up sunlight on cool mornings. The sail could have helped it lose heat on hot days.

Spinosaurus lived in North Africa. The days were hot, and the nights were cool.

Giganotosaurus lived in South America.

Giganotosaurus did not have a sail on its back. But it was also huge. Its name means "giant lizard of the south."

Who Was the Biggest?

People learn about dinosaurs by studying fossils. Fossils are the remains of animals that lived long ago.

Bones become fossils when they are buried in sand or mud. Tracks can also become fossils.

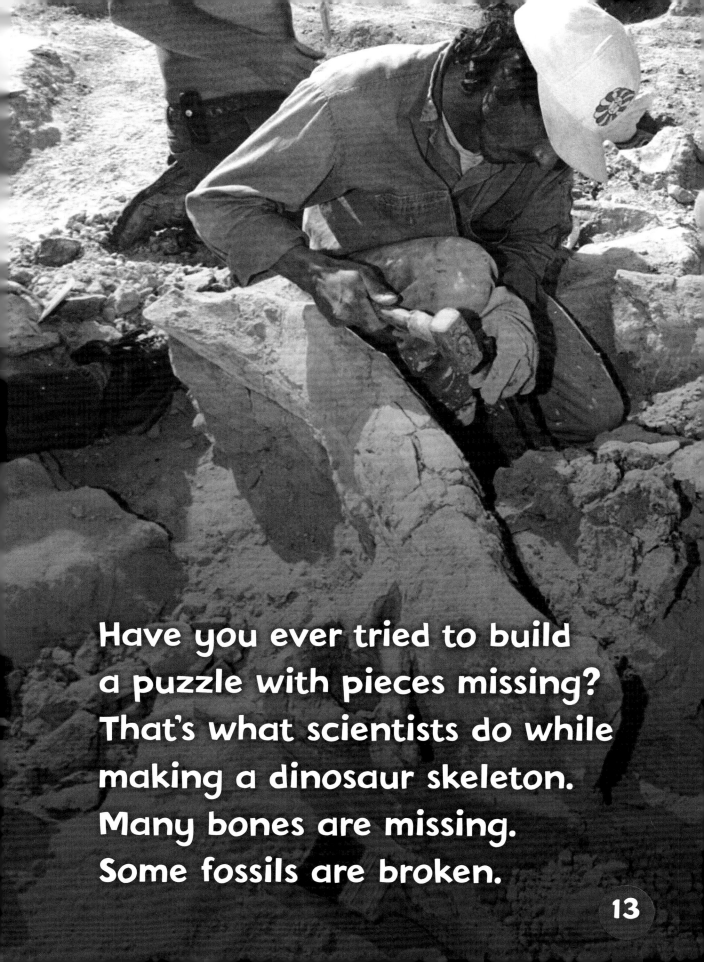

Have you ever tried to build
a puzzle with pieces missing?
That's what scientists do while
making a dinosaur skeleton.
Many bones are missing.
Some fossils are broken.

No one knows the exact size of many dinosaurs. So scientists piece together fossils. They measure different bones. That helps them figure out a dinosaur's size.

This Spinosaurus skull was almost 6 feet (1.8 meters) long. You could fit inside it!

Giganotosaurus might have been the heaviest meat eater. It weighed about as much as a school bus.

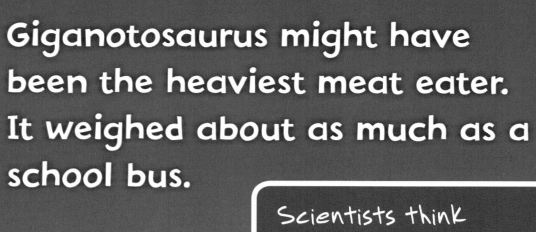

Scientists think Giganotosaurus was as long as a school bus too.

Spinosaurus was probably not as heavy as Giganotosaurus. But it might have been the longest theropod.

Some scientists think it grew as long as a volleyball court.

Sharp Teeth

Meat eaters needed sharp teeth. Pointed teeth could grip prey. Some teeth cut like knives. Others crushed bones.

Giganotosaurus teeth were the size of bananas. They had sharp points and flat, jagged edges. They cut through skin.

Spinosaurus had sharp, cone-shaped teeth. Its teeth did not have jagged edges.

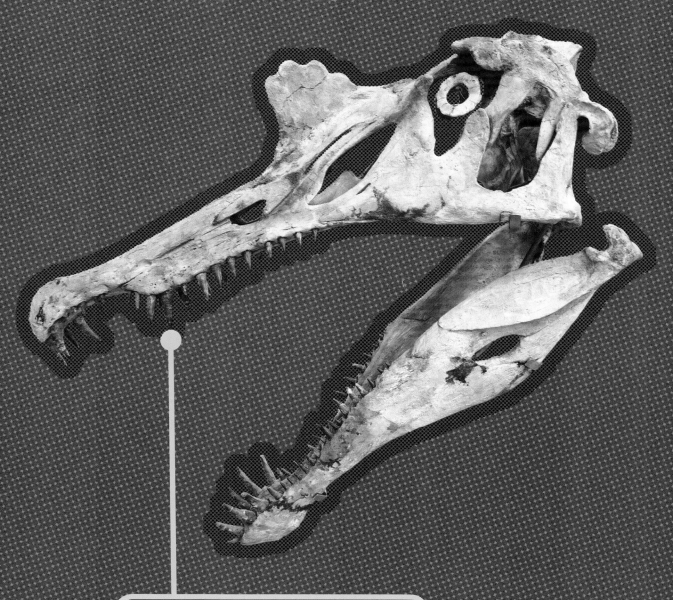

Spinosaurus teeth were shorter than Giganotosaurus teeth.

Giganotosaurus could bite hard. Strong muscles helped its jaws snap shut.

Giganotosaurus had more than sixty teeth.

Eighty teeth lined Spinosaurus's big jaws.

Spinosaurus's snout was longer than Giganotosaurus's snout. Its skull was shaped like a crocodile's skull.

On the Hunt

Giganotosaurus searched for food on land. It sniffed out prey with its nose.

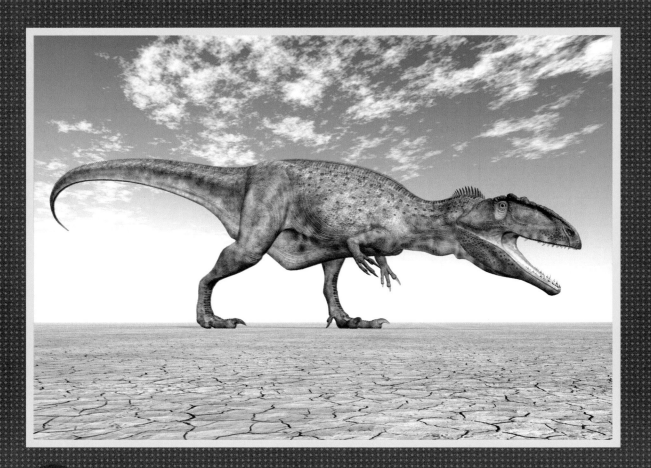

Spinosaurus probably hunted in rivers. Its eyes were high and far back on its skull. It could look around while floating in water.

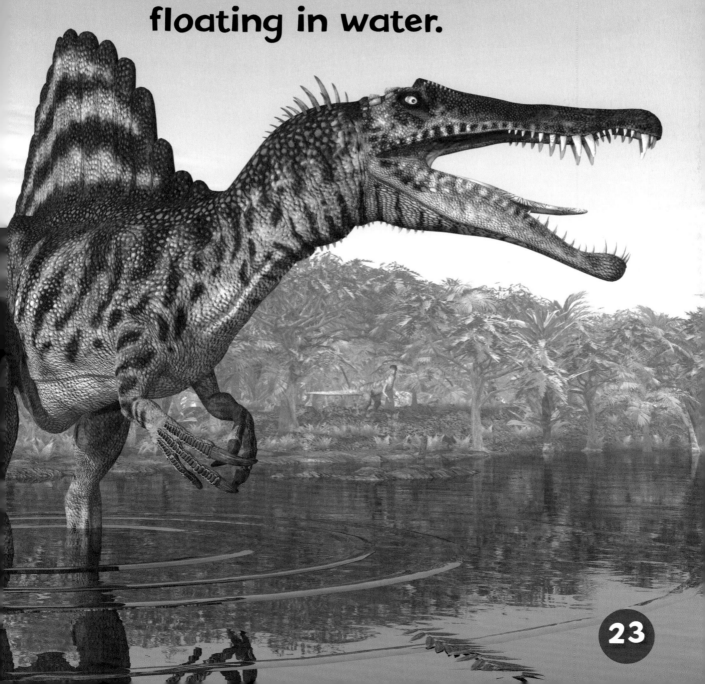

Huge plant-eating dinosaurs
lived near Giganotosaurus.
Giganotosaurus might have
hunted these giants. Their
fossils have been found near
Giganotosaurus bones.

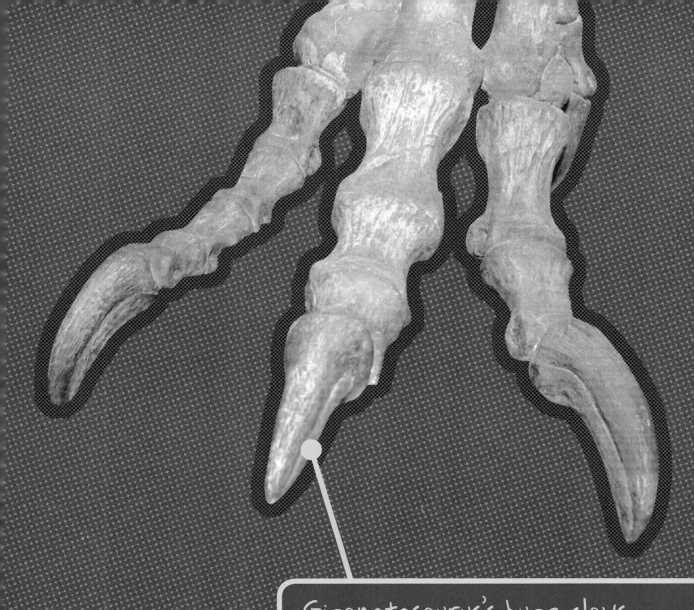

Giganotosaurus's huge claws helped it attack large animals.

How did Giganotosaurus catch its prey? Scientists wonder if it hunted in groups.

Spinosaurus probably found fish in the water. Its sharp teeth were good for fishing. Its claws might have hooked fish.

Fish parts have been found with Spinosaurus fossils.

Spinosaurus might have hunted on land too. Its teeth could not slice open giant dinosaurs. But it could have trapped and eaten smaller prey.

Dino Diagrams

Can you tell these dinosaurs apart?

Giganotosaurus

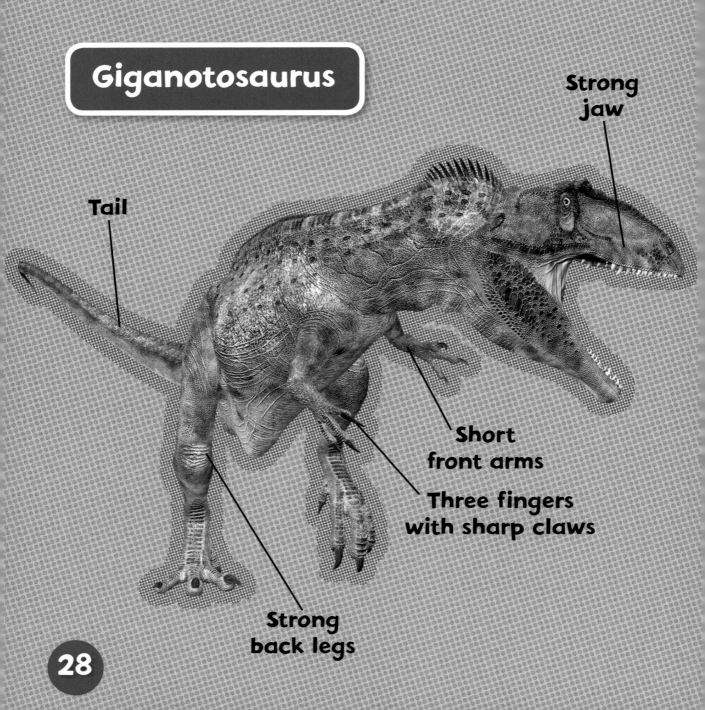

Strong jaw

Tail

Short front arms

Three fingers with sharp claws

Strong back legs

Spinosaurus

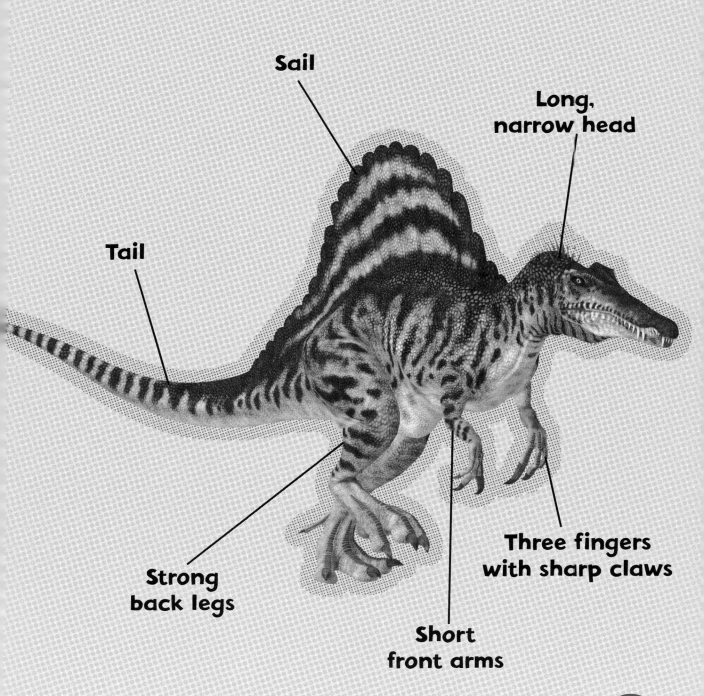

Sail

Long,
narrow head

Tail

Strong
back legs

Short
front arms

Three fingers
with sharp claws

29

Glossary

fossil: the remains of a living thing from a long time ago

prey: an animal that is eaten by another animal

sail: the spines and skin on the back of Spinosaurus or a similar animal

skeleton: the inner structure of an animal with a backbone

skull: the part of a skeleton that protects the parts inside an animal's head

theropod: a group of meat-eating dinosaurs that walked on their back legs and had short front arms

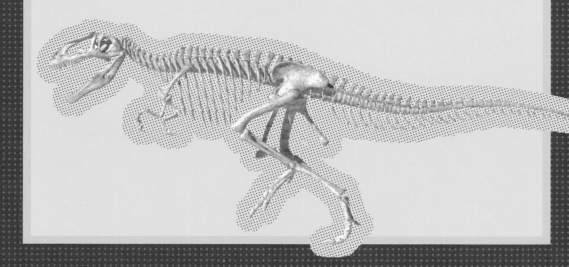

Further Reading

Brecke, Nicole, and Patricia M. Stockland. *Dinosaurs and Other Prehistoric Creatures You Can Draw.* Minneapolis: Millbrook Press, 2010.

Dinosaurs—Natural History Museum
http://www.nhm.ac.uk/kids-only/dinosaurs/index.html

Giganotosaurus—TheDinosaurs.org
http://www.thedinosaurs.org/dinosaurs/giganotosaurus.aspx

Lessem, Don. *National Geographic Kids Ultimate Dinopedia: The Most Complete Dinosaur Reference Ever.* Washington, DC: National Geographic, 2010.

Paleontology: The Big Dig—American Natural History Museum
http://www.amnh.org/explore/ology/paleontology

Shone, Rob. *Giganotosaurus: The Giant Southern Lizard.* New York: Rosen Publishing Group, 2009.

Spinosaurus Facts for Kids—Science Kids
http://www.sciencekids.co.nz/sciencefacts/dinosaurs/spinosaurus.html

Index

Photo Acknowledgments

The images in this book are used with the permission of: © Elle Arden Images/ Shutterstock.com, pp. 1 (top), 9; © Michael Rosskothen/Shutterstock.com, pp. 1 (bottom), 7 (both), 11, 22, 28; © Andreas Meyer/Dreamstime.com, pp. 2, 21; © Stocktrek Images/ SuperStock, pp. 4, 23; © Sukram-C/flickr.com, p. 5; Didier Descouens (CC-BY-SA-3.0), pp. 6, 19; © Kabacchi/flickr.com, pp. 8, 17; © Kostyantyn Ivanyshen/Shutterstock.com, p. 10; © Maria Stenzel/National Geographic/Getty Images, p. 12; RICKEY ROGERS/ Reuters/Newscom, p. 13; © FRANCK ROBICHON/epa/CORBIS, p. 14; © NHPA/SuperStock, p. 15; © Sofia Santos/Shutterstock.com, p. 16; © Todd Strand/Independent Picture Service, p. 18; Design Pics/ Peter Langer/Newscom, p. 20; © James L. Amos/Science Source, p. 24; © Reuters/CORBIS, p. 25; iStockphoto.com/Adrian Chesterman, p. 26; © Mair5400/Dreamstime.com, p. 27; © Ralf Kraft/Dreamstime.com, p. 29; © Leonello Calvetti/Shutterstock.com, p. 30.

Front Cover: © Corey A. Ford/Dreamstime.com (bottom); © Linda Bucklin/Dreamstime. com (top).

Main body text set in Johann Light 30/36.

Atlanta-Fulton Public Library